MW01253848

ANGER MANAGEMENT SKILLS FOR CHILDREN

FOR THE TEENAGER

IDA GREENE, Ph.D.

Anger Management Skills for Teenagers. Copyright © March 27, 2008; P. S. I. Publishers, 2910 Baily Ave. San Diego, CA 92105. All rights reserved. No part of this publication may be reproduced, distributed, transmitted, transcribed, stored in a retrieval system, or translated into any language without the express prior agreement and written permission of the publisher. Other books by the author are: Self-Esteem the Essence of You, Success Now, Soft Power Negotiation SkillsTM, How to Be a Success In Business, and Light The Fire Within You.

ISBN 1-8865-23-X

ATTENTION COLLEGES AND UNIVERSITIES, CORPORATIONS, AND PROFESSIONAL ORGANIZATIONS: Quantity discounts are available on bulk purchases of this book for educational training purposes, fund raising, or gift giving. For information contact: **P. S. I. Publishers, 2910 Baily Ave. San Diego, CA 92105 (619) 262-9951.**

FOREWORD

We are feeling, caring, and reacting persons, which is good. The problem is that we sometimes overreact, react at the wrong time, or react in a manner that hurts others.

Hopefully, this workbook will be a useful tool to help you respond appropriately to others; so that your verbal communication, physical communication (body language) and your emotional communication is experienced in a pleasant manner.

All emotions are good, your interactions and communication patterns will determine how people will think about you, feel about you, or how they will respond to you.

ACKNOWLEDGEMENTS

I give thanks for both the good and unpleasant encounters I have experienced. I give thanks for the pleasant and unpleasant people I have met, I have learned from both.

Some life lessons can be taught and other lessons have to be bought through your trial and error, pain and hardship.

Hopefully you will be a student of life and learn from the mistakes of others.

I wish to thank Catherine Bozigian for creating the charts in this book.

Ida Greene, Ph.D.

Chapter 1

ANGER MANAGEMENT CONCEPTS FOR THE TEENAGER

One thing that any child can do to enhance their self-esteem is to be in control of all toxic emotions. A toxic emotion is any emotion that has the potential to cause harm to another person, create disharmony between you and another, to be a source of conflict, cause irreparable damage to a relationship, or to destroy an interaction between you and another. Anger can be like an atomic bomb when uncontrolled.

The following are emotions I consider toxic: Envy, Jealousy, Revenge, Fear, Hatred, and Anger. All of these emotions are addressed extensively in the book, "Light the Fire Within You". Anger will be discussed here because it is often the cause of problems between you and others.

Anger is a powerful emotion and you get to decide if you will express or suppress it. Anger is a chosen position. We can decide how we will react to a perceived threat to our ego, or emotional comfort. Anger is a signal for you, to look at what is going on in your emotions, to find the cause of your frustration or confusion.

Anger can be used by others to confuse or control you. In conflict resolution, anger is a useful emotion when used to support yourself against attacks by others to over power or control you. Anger takes away energy, because it negatively charges your emotions, even when it is used constructively. Anger must be under your control at all times, because of its potential to hurt or destroy others self-confidence.

Conflict resolution Anger is useful when it is used to prevent you from being abused by others. Anger is always a loss of energy.

However, anger is a valuable signal, because it lets us know when something is wrong and needs to be corrected.

The critical factor is for you to decide whether your expression of anger will add to or solve your problem. An explosive outburst of anger rarely solves a problem. It usually makes the situation worse and leaves you having to apologize for your behavior. An unexpected angry outburst often frightens people and causes them to be afraid of you and your unpredictable expression of emotions

Anger is a valuable signal, because it lets us know when something is wrong and needs to be corrected. The critical factor is whether your expression of anger is adding to the problem rather than solving your problem.

Often when we are angry, one or more of these things are going on:
1. We want something and are not getting it.
2. We expect trouble, based on our past experiences.
3. We feel powerless to get what we want.

The premise of anger management techniques is for you to use your anger as a signal to identify your problem and deal with it. Rather than act upon your anger by lashing out or to hold your angry feelings inside.

YOUR SELF-CONCEPT/SELF-IDENTITY
Is composed of:
* A **thought** is an unspoken word
* A **word** is a spoken thought
* Behavior is **a thought** and **word**

Our thoughts, words create our behavior. Children struggle on a daily basis to maintain their identity or sense of self. We must like respect, and appreciate ourselves before they can like and respect another person. Children are open and loving; yet lack the skills to nurture, protect, or maintain their sense of self against subtle or open bias, intimidation, rejection and anger. Anger is our body's response to a perceived insult, hurt, emotional pain, shame or humiliation. We all want and need to feel good about ourselves. We do not like to be belittled, humiliated are made to feel small or inferior. When we are hurt, we may feel the need to retaliate or defend ourselves. We show our feelings of displeasure through the emotion of anger. We rarely become angry with those we trust.

A DEFINITION OF ANGER

Everybody has his or her own definition of anger. Webster's New World Dictionary defines anger as *a noun, a feeling of shame or displeasure, resulting from injury, mistreatment, opposition. It usually shows itself in a desire to fight back at the supposed cause of discomfort.*

We Define Anger As:

- An **emotion**, that is physically arousing with unique physiological correlates.
- A **feeling**. It has an effect on the way you experience your world.
- A **communicator**. Anger sends information to others.
- A **cause**. Anger produces specific effects and results.

Write About Your Definition of Anger.

....

....

....

Descriptive words to understand myself better are:

1. ....

2. ....

3. ....

4. ....

....

Anger is triggered by external events called provocations, which creates arousal, anger thoughts and angry actions, which escalate each other until they are fused together like the three prongs of a pitch fork, in an anger feedback loop that leads to destructive consequences. the more intense the anger feedback loop, the harder it is to break. As the center of the triangle gets smaller, the tension/fusion increases.

TRUST ME!

Five people I trust are

- ....

- ....

- ....

- ....

- ....

I trust them because ....

....

....

....

I think ....(number) people trust me.

They trust me because ....

....

....

....

I can earn other people's trust by ....

....

....

....

6

IF I COULD CHANGE MY APPEARANCE

Some people aren't happy with the way they look and want to change a few things about themselves. Maybe you don't like the way your body looks or the size of your feet. Draw what you look like now in one box and in the other; draw what you want to look like.

ME NOW   HOW I WANT TO BE

MY PERFECT FAMILY

If you could change your family, what would it look like? Draw yourself at the larger circle, and the rest of your ideal family in the other circles. Then on the lines below, write why you would like each person to be in your family.

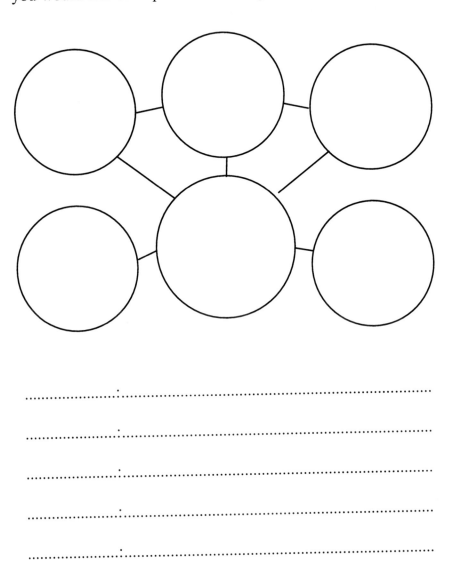

MY REAL FAMILY

In the spaces below, write the the names of five members of your family. Across from their name, tell what you like to do with that person.

FAMILY MEMBER
Example: Mom

WHAT I LIKE TO DO WITH THEM
Example: Play games, dance

1. _____

1. _____

_____

2. _____

2. _____

_____

3. _____

3. _____

_____

4. _____

4. _____

_____

5. _____

5. _____

_____

HOUSE RULES
Answer the questions below.

1. What objects in your house are you not allowed to touch?

....

....

2. What happens if you touch something you're not allowed?

....

....

....

3. What things are you not allowed to do, by yourself?

— ....

....

....

4. What things are you allowed to do, by yourself?

....

....

....

5. Why do you think parents make these rules?

a. ....

b. ....

MY DUTIES

In the spaces below list four duties you have at school and at home. Use the numbers below to indicate how dependable you are in doing your duties.

1 = poor; 2 = fair; 3 = good; 4 = excellent

School Duties	**Rating**
1.	....
2.	....
3.	....
4.	....
....	....

Home Duties	**Rating**
1.	....
2.	....
3.	....
4.	....

NECESSARY RULES

Answer the questions below.

1. What would your house be like if you didn't have rules?

....

....

....

2. What would school be like if we didn't have rules?

....

....

....

3. If you were the teacher, what rules would you make for the class? List the three most important rules.

a. ....

b. ....

c. ....

4. Would you make rules against hurting people's feelings? What would be some good rules?

....

....

....

5. What would be the punishment for breaking the rules?

....

....

....

My New Rules

Answer the questions below:

1. What rules should be set for younger brothers and sisters to follow?..
    ....
    ....

2. What rules should be set for older brothers and sisters to follow? ....
    ....

3. What new rules would you make for your family?
    ....
    ....

4. What new rules would you set for your school?
    ....
    ....

5. What new rules would you set for children and adults to follow? ....
    ....
    ....

6. If children and adults followed the same rules, what would it be like? ....
    ....
    ....

THE CLASSROOM

Answer the questions below:

1. In which ways is the classroom like a family?

   ....
   ....
   ....

2. What type of members of the family is there? Who is the parent?

   ....
   ....
   ....

3. List how a school is like a society.

   ....
   ....
   ....

4. 4.If you were the ruler of the class, would you make it a dictatorship, democracy, or a monarchy?

   ....
   ....
   ....
   ....

You Can Count On Me!

We all count upon others for certain things. How do you count on these people and what do they count on you for? Complete the blanks below.

I count on Mom or Dad for	I count on my teacher for
_____	_____
_____	_____
	.
My Mom or Dad counts on me to	My teacher counts on me to
_____	_____
_____	_____
I count on my friend for	I count on my brother or sister for
_____	
_____	_____
My friend counts on me for	He or she counts on me to
_____	_____
_____	_____

Story Time

Write a short story including all of the characters below. Talk about what they do together, if they get along, and what they might fight about.

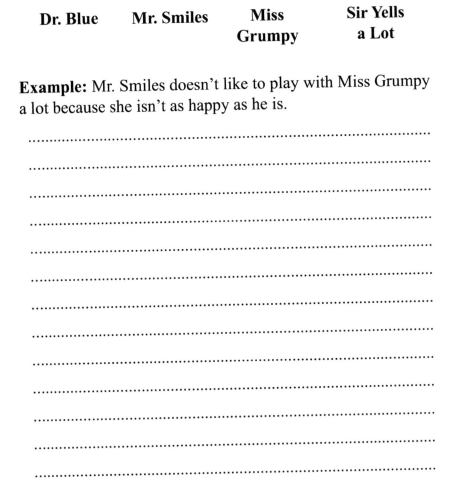

| Dr. Blue | Mr. Smiles | Miss Grumpy | Sir Yells a Lot |

Example: Mr. Smiles doesn't like to play with Miss Grumpy a lot because she isn't as happy as he is.

....

....

....

....

....

....

....

....

....

....

....

....

WHAT I WANTED

Everyone has wanted something special. Maybe you wanted a dog or a new game. Sometimes, when we don't get these things, we feel bad. Answer the questions below about what you felt like when you didn't get what you wanted.

The special thing I wanted was:	I wanted it because:............. ....
What did you want it for? (Birthday, holidays, etc.)	Who did you want to do it? ....
Why didn't you get it?	Were you mad? ....

The next time I don't get what I want, instead of feeling mad, I'm going to:

....

....

....

....

DRAW IT!

Choose two people you know – they could be family members, friends or even teachers. Draw one picture of what they look like when they're happy and another of when they're mad. Then circle which picture of each person that you like better.

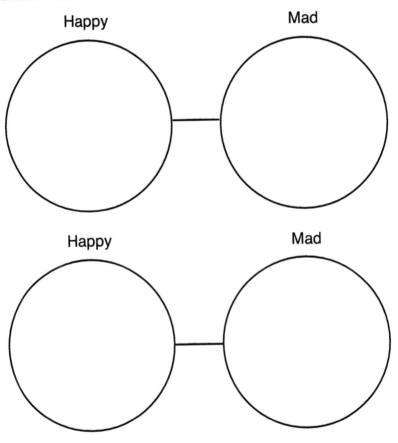

A Glance into the Future
Complete the sentences below.

1. I want to become ....
....

2. When I graduate from college I would like to ....
....
....

3. When I'm an adult, I think I would like to ....
....
....

4. To be what I want to be when I'm an adult, I'll need to
learn about ....
....

5. If I could change myself, I'd like to be more...................
....
and less ....
....

6. If I could move to anywhere in the world, it would be to
....

7. I would like to take these things or people with me when
I move ....
....
....

TEN YEARS FROM NOW

As people get older, a lot of things change about them. They may have a different hair color or a different job.

Pretend that you are ten years older and imagine what life would be like. Draw a picture of what you think you would look like in ten years and also write about how your ideas may have changed since you were in school.

....

....

....

....

....

....

....

....

Discourtesy is the beginnings of violence.

Chapter 2

HOW TO BE IN CONTROL OF YOURSELF

One thing that any child can do to enhance their self-esteem is to be in control of all toxic emotions. A toxic emotion is any emotion that has the potential to cause harm to another person, create disharmony between you and another, to be a source of conflict, cause irreparable damage to a relationship, or to destroy an interaction between you and another.

The following are emotions I consider toxic: Envy, Jealousy, Revenge, Fear, Hatred, and Anger. All of these emotions are addressed extensively in the book, *Light the Fire Within You.* Anger will be discussed here because it is often the cause of problems between you and others.

Anger is a chosen position. We can decide how we will react to a perceived threat to our ego, or emotional comfort. Anger is a signal for you, to look at what is going on in your emotions, and to find the cause of the anger.

Anger can be used by others to confuse or control you. In conflict resolution, anger is a useful emotion when used to support yourself against attacks by others to over power or control you. Anger takes away energy, because it emotionally charges you, even when used constructively. Because of its potential to hurt or destroy others self-confidence, anger must be under your control. Anger can be like an atomic bomb when uncontrolled.

Often when we are angry, one or more of these are going on:

1. We want something and are not getting it.
2. From past experience we expect trouble.
3. We have feelings of powerlessness.
4. We feel sadness.
5. Feelings of grief, which take away our joy and liveliness.
6. Depression.
7. Feelings of negativity about life, self, and people.

Always assume responsibility for what you are feeling, and own all your feelings, including anger. Unresolved anger turns into resentment, envy, jealousy, revenge, and hatred. There is always an underlying feeling of inadequacy when you are angry.

Anger moves through the following stages if it is not resolved immediately:

Frustration → Disappointment Over Unmet Needs → Embarrassment → Guilt → Fear of Rejection

1. **Frustration** – unfulfilled expectations. Solution: change your goal or plan.
2. **Unmet Needs/Disappointment** – your unfulfilled expectations. Solution: look into the situation and get the facts.
3. **Embarrassment** – expected self-image unfulfilled. Solution: create new self-image.
4. **Guilt** – social expectations you have accepted. Solution: confront the situation behavior or change it.
5. **Fear of rejection** – unknown expectations with probability of consequence. Solution: confront the situation/person/ behavior, explore the cause then decide if you want to avoid the behavior that causes the problem.

Anger is a waste of energy, because it takes away your joy. It can be used by others to confuse or control you if you are unaware of what you are feeling, unclear about what angers you, or have no control over your anger outbursts. In conflict resolution, anger is a useful emotion when used to support yourself against an attack by others to over power or control you.

Learning to Control Your Anger Will Help You:
1. Recognize your temper, mood, or state of mind.
2. Validate your temperament.
3. Learn to delay action on your temper.
4. Label and verbalize your feelings.
5. Think about your options.
6. Empathize with others, and apologize if necessary.

ANGER, THE DEMON INSIDE US
First of all, we have two basic ways of dealing with our anger, We can prevent it, i.e. keep anger from welling up inside of us, or control it, i.e. modify our aggressive urges after anger erupts inside. The preventative approach is ideal – Avoid frustrating situations, be assertive when things first annoy you, eliminate irrational ideas that arouse you to anger. Realize that we can not avoid all frustrations and thoughts that arouse us to anger..

Secondly, in the situations where we have not, learned to prevent an angry reaction, we fall into two easily recognized categories: (a) Repressors--Suppressor or (b) Exploders "hot-headed expressers". See if you can recognize yourself and others you are close to in these categories. The person who represses or suppresses anger have not prevented the anger, they have just hidden or suppressed it. The repressor or suppressor may eventually erupt in fits of rage, much like the "exploders. However, in "exploders," angry feelings and aggressive responses are immediate and there is little time for prevention, or time to think about avoiding getting angry, the emotions just spew out, venting feelings, and assertiveness may be helpful. Exploders could use the same methods including learning tolerance, challenging irrational ideas to strengthen their feelings of love and compassion.

To help you manage your anger better focus more on gentle and kind thoughts designed to build self-esteem. Learn to model non-aggressive behavioral responses, and reward constructive non-violent behavior. There are times when anger is appropriate and effective. Carol Tavris, in her research papers of 1984, says anger is more effective it is directed at the offending person or the expression of anger satisfies your need to correct an injustice.

Sometimes the best thing to do about anger is nothing, including thinking nothing about the incident. The irritating event is often unimportant and its memory will soon fade away; if you stay quiet and the relationship stays respectful. Some theorists say that mental self-instructions to suppress anger for a long period of time may be risky, because it lowers our self-esteem, increases our sense of powerlessness, and increases our health risks. Other theorists point to a phenomenon called "laughter in church," i.e. holding back the expression of an emotion with laughing may strengthen the feeling of anger; watch for these problems if you hold back your feelings. If you have suppressed the emotional outburst but the anger still rages inside, you may need to vent the anger privately. The person who can suppress a moment's anger may prevent a day of sorrow for themselves or another.

Use your problem-solving skills; try out different approaches to see how they work. If you are a yeller and screamer, try quiet tolerance and daily visualization techniques mentioned in this book. If you are a name-caller, try using "I" statements, like *"I am feeling very angry right now,"* or *"I do not want to talk right now,"* or *"I need to cool off /chill"*. If you sulk and withdraw for hours, try saying, *"I have a problem I'd like to talk about soon."* If you tend to strike out with your fists, try hitting a punching bag until you can find a reasonable verbal approach to solve the problem. Baron and others have shown that some behavioral responses are incompatible with getting intensely angry and seem to help us calm down. Responses like empathy, giving the offender a gift, or asking for sympathy, or responding with humor or asking the offending person to clarify her or his perceived insult.

In addition to incompatible overt responses, there are many covert or internal responses you might use that will help suppress or control your anger. Examples: Mental self-instructions to yourself, like: *"they are just trying to make me mad,"* or *"don't lose control and start yelling,"* may influence greatly your view of the situation and be helpful for you to avoid and control your aggression. Some of the major methods for Anger control we use in our groups are: Relaxation, Rational-Emotive (reasoning and emotional) techniques, Self-Talk, Self-Instructions and Stress-Reduction methods.

Stop hostile fantasies. Preoccupation with the irritating situation, including repeatedly talking about it, may only increase your anger. Instead try thought stopping to punish your anger-generating fantasies or substitute rewarding constructive how-to-improve-the-situation thoughts, like: *"I am too busy to hate, I am absorbed in something bigger than myself,"* or *"I* *have no time to quarrel, no time for regrets, and no one can force me to stoop low enough to argue or fight with them."*

Guard against escalating violence. When we are mad, we frequently are attempting to over exaggerate, hurt the person who we feel has hurt us a lot more. There are two problems with retaliating with anger to a perceived hurt. The person may be tempted to counterattack you even more vigorously and you will probably start thinking of them more negatively (in order to convince yourself that he/she deserved the severe punishment you gave him/her) which makes you want to aggress again. Thus, the saying, "violence breeds violence" is true. Violence produces more hate in your opponent and in you. Research has shown that controlled, moderate retaliation so that "things are equal" in contrast to "teaching people a lesson" feels better in the long run than excessive retaliation. It is best to walk away from an argument and let the other person have the last word.

Record the antecedents and consequences of your anger. As with all behaviors, you need to know (a) the learning history of your angry reactions behavior. What happened before you became angry and what happened after. Your approach to others is likely to change the other person's behavior, which means you can express yourself in a way so they can understand your point of view and want to cooperate with you.

Sometimes it is best to "bite your lip" or "hold your tongue" and vent your anger privately (by yourself) or to forget it. You will be surprised how often the suppression of hot, vile, cutting remarks avoids a nasty scene. Both prevention-of-anger and control-of-anger methods are given in this section. Learn to reduce your frustrations. You know who makes you mad, what topics of conversation upset you, the situations that drive you up a wall. Try to avoid them? This could be the best way to prevent anger. Even if you can't permanently avoid a person whom you currently dislike, staying away from that person for a few days could reduce the anger.

You may need to clarify or change your goals. Having no goals can be uncomfortable. Having impossible goals can be infuriating. You may need to plan ways to surmount the barriers that stand in your way. Learn to reduce the environmental support for your aggression. How aggressive, mean, and nasty we are is partly determined by the behavior of those around us (Aronson, 1984). Perhaps you can avoid subcultures of violence, such as gangs or friends who are hostile, TV violence, or action movies. More importantly, select as your friends people who are not quick tempered or cruel and not agitators or prejudiced. Examples: if you are in high school and see your friends being very disrespectful and belligerent with teachers or parents, you are more likely to become the same way. So, choose your friends carefully. Pleasant, tactful role models as friends are very important

Explain yourself and understand others. This can make a big difference in the other persons' understanding of you.. So, if you are getting irritated at someone for being inconsiderate of you, ask them if something is wrong, or say, "*I'm sorry you are having a hard time.*" Similarly, if you are having a bad day and feeling grouchy, ask others (in advance) to excuse you because you are upset. This can changes the environment for both you and the other person.

Develop better ways of behaving. Although we may feel like hitting the other person and cursing them out, using our most degrading and vile language, we usually realize this would be unwise. Research confirms that calmly expressed anger is far more understandable and tolerable than an emotional tirade.

ANGER MANAGEMENT – BASIC CONCEPTS

To Change Your Expression of Anger, You Must Change Your Thinking

RETHINK
Change what you say to yourself in your head, in response to the external event.

1. Anger is a powerful emotion.
2. Reason is not employed when we are angry.
3. Anger is the results of jumping to conclusions about an outcome.
4. Anger creates a sense of energy, excitement and negative aliveness
5. Anger is self-serving
6. Anger is addictive/obsessive thinking you can't let go.
7. Anger is about power and control
8. Anger is used to scare, instill fear in others and as an outlet to get rid of the negative inner feelings you do not know how to handle.
9. You do not have the right to hurt another person with your anger.
10. No one has given you permission to hurt them because of your inability to handle your problems.
11. When you are angry, you are out of control, not the other person.
12. Others may provoke you to anger, but you do not have to respond angrily. When you respond as others want, they have the power to control you.
13. No one is the cause of you responding angrily. You have freedom of choice.
14. When you get mad, you are exercising your power, or you seek to avenge yourself.

15. You get some pleasure from hurting others, if you get angry repeatedly.
16. If you get angry often, you are unable to control your feelings.
17. Anger is a powerful emotion, either you control it, or you are controlled by it.

Draw a picture of your anger:

ANGER TRIGGERS

The Major Causes of Anger Are:
1. Grief – Loss-Past/Present/Future
2. Sadness → Hurt → Emotional Pain
3. Resentment → Envy →Hate
4. Victim Mind Set – Lack of boundaries
5. Abuse – a. Deep dependency needs; b. Revenge
6. Low Self-Esteem – a. Jealousy; b. Envy
7. Fear – of the Unknown/Rejection
8. Unmet Needs – a. Nurturance; b. Low Self-Worth
9. Unfulfilled Expectations – Loneliness

The Secondary Causes of Anger:
1. Stress.
2. Desire to have or be in control of things.
3. Intolerance to criticism.
4. Chronic deficit of attention or recognition.
5. Feelings of abandonment.
6. Feelings of rejection.
7. Fragile emotions/low ego strength (inability to recognize or accept one's faults).
8. Antagonistic/Argumentative disposition.
9. Feelings of narcissism.
10. Superiority/Inferiority complex – "Be Perfect Script"

When you develop inner control of a powerful emotion like anger, you become powerful. When your outer environment controls you, you lose the opportunity to have inner control. To become good at any skill, whether it is controlling your expression of anger or your tongue, it requires continuous practice.

TEN STEPS TO CONTROL YOUR ANGER:

1. Make a list of the things that make you mad, and memorize it.

2. Talk about your feelings, tell people when things bother you.

3. When you feel angry, do something with the energy. Slowly breathe in and out ten times. On the exhale, spread you fingers widely apart and imagine the negative energy leaving your body as you do so.

4. When you feel the urge to strike out at someone, shrug (raise) your shoulders, as you breathe in deeply; rapidly lower your shoulders as you exhale. Notice your jaw muscles, shoulders, hands, chest, torso muscles. Get in touch with what you are angry about, and with whom you are angry.

5. Make peace with yourself and the person who is the object of your anger. Forgive yourself first, and then apologize to the other person for your lack of control.

6. Mentally visualize two paths, (there is an exercise in the book *Light the Fire Within You,* that teaches you how to visualize. Have one of these paths be positive, pleasant, and full of light. Have the other path be dark, gloomy, and depressing. Then send your angry feelings down the dark path and over the cliff.

7. Notice if you feel like yelling, screaming, or hitting. Before you act on your anger, think of why you are angry.

Is your feeling legitimate or did you create a situation to justify your anger?

8. Talk your way through your anger. Tell yourself you can change from being a reactor of your emotions to being a processor. Notice your thoughts; change negative thoughts into positive ones.

9. Change the image you have of yourself from "blowing your stack" to being a "cool headed person." Whenever you are able to control your anger, reinforce it by saying something kind to yourself.

10. Daily seek ways to change your image, inner thoughts, and outer behavior, so the two match.

Additional Things You Can Do to Control Anger:

11. See yourself as a kind person.

12. Seek to become a thinker rather than an emotional reactor. To be an emotional reactor is to be out of control. An emotional reactor, discharges and wastes valuable energy needed by the brain to process information. When you are an emotional reactor you deplete your body of vital minerals and nutrients.

13. Pay attention to your feelings. Remember to validate your feelings by asking yourself these questions: "What am I feeling?" "Why am I feeling this way?" "What were the circumstances that caused me to feeling this way?" "How often do I feel this way?" and "Who am I emulating?"

14. Work through negative emotions as soon as they emerge. Listen to hear what the other person is saying to you. When in doubt, ask for clarification.
16. Listen with the intent to understand. Repeat back to the other person in your words what you think you heard.
17. Notice your body, its space, the body of others and their space.
18. Give others freedom of space and they will honor your space.

SUGGESTIONS FOR SELF CONTROL AND SELF DISCIPLINE:

1. Learn to organize your immediate environment.

2. Put things back as you find them to help create order and stability for yourself.

3. Strive to be the same all the time

4. Learn to organize your life by keeping a daily list of things you plan to do – a *To Do List*. List your daily activities into A, B, C, D categories. 'A' represents activities with the highest priority.

5. Never settle for less than your best effort, best preparation, and best outcome, then your best follow-through.

6. Be your own coach, encourage yourself by saying and thinking positively.

7. Push yourself to be your best, and tell yourself you can.

8. Others may provoke you to anger, but you do not have to respond angrily.

9. When you do what others want, they are in control of you.

10. No one is the cause of you responding angrily. You have freedom of choice to behave and respond as you choose.

11. When you get mad, you are trying to protect your ego and self-pride.

12. If you get angry repeatedly, you get some pleasure from hurting others

13. If you get angry repeatedly, you are unable to control your feelings of frustration and have a need to "get even" to hurt as you feel you were hurt.

14. To keep your anger under control, do a kind act each day for yourself and another person.

15. Give yourself permission to be kind to yourself and others.

16. Find ways to be gentle, and kind to yourself and others

17. Breathe deeply often during the day to release tension and stress.

18. Work on being the same on both inside and outside yourself

19. Learn to meditate, (sit still, think on pleasant thought of nature) for one minutes, two times a day. Dr. Ida Greene lists the techniques in her book, *Light The Fire Within You*™

Have you ever felt any of the emotions below? How do they make you feel about yourself? *Go through the exercises below to be in better control of your emotions Write about when you felt the feelings below toward someone.*

• **Anger:** ....
....
....

• **Revenge:** ....
....
....

• **Jealousy:** ....
....
....

• **Resentment:** ....
....
....

How did you feel after you expressed the emotions above?

a. Did you feel happy, tired, or sad? *Write about your feelings, now.* ....
....
....

b. If you felt good, why? ....
....
....

c. Do you feel good when you hurt others?

....

....

d. How do you feel when others hurt you? ....

....

....

Write the words you use when talking with others about your anger.

....

....

For one week, monitor your inner self-talk and outer behavior. Write down your bodily reactions: breathing, clenched teeth, heavy breathing, tight neck or shoulder muscles, tight jaws, hot ears or other body parts, rigid, tense body posture, balled fist, rolled eyes.

Day 1 ....

....

Day 2 ....

....

Day 3 ....

....

Day 4 ....

....

Day 5 ....

....

Day 6 ....

....

Day 7 ....

....

COMPLETE THE LISTS BELOW:

1. List the people to whom you can go when you need help.

   ....

   ....

2. List the reference books you know how to use (dictionary, Encyclopedia).

   ....

   ....

3. List the places in your city where you can call on the phone or go for information.

   ....

   ....

   ....

4. List four questions you would like to know the answers but don't know where to get information.

   ....

   ....

   ....

   ....

   ....

   ....

   ....

   ....

   ....

   ....

AN EXERCISE TO UNDERSTAND ANGER BETTER

Circle the word(s) or number(s) that best fit you.

1. I would describe myself as a *nice* | *smart* | *angry* | *happy* person.

2. Others would describe me as a *nice* | *smart* | *angry* | *happy* person.

3. I get angry *1-5* | *5-10* | *10-20* times a day.

4. When I'm angry I *cry* | *scream* | *don't talk*.

5. This person makes me angry a lot *mom/dad* | *brother/sister* | *friend* | *teacher*.

6. They make me angry because they don't *listen to me* | *let me do what I want* | *care about me*.

7. When I get mad, they *ignore me* | *get mad at me* | *make me feel better*.

8. When I'm angry, I feel *better* | *worse* | *the same* than when I'm happy.

9. What makes me feel better when I'm angry is *talking about why I'm angry* | *playing/singing/dancing* | *ignoring the problem*.

10. I *do* | *don't* like myself when I'm angry.

ANGER MANAGEMENT ASSESSMENT

1. What is your definition of anger? Write it out. Is it a good feeling or a bad feeling?

    ....

    ....

2. Describe your bodily reactions e.g.. tightness of throat: what part of your body, muscle grouping, do you feel the emotion of anger?

    ....

    ....

    ....

3. Are you able to think about your body reactions when you are angry?

    ....

4. Are you able to think about what caused you to get/be angry, when you are angry? Write about this.

    ....

    ....

5. What do you feel when you are angry? Select one word or phrase below and explain why you selected it.

    A. Out of control; B. Powerful; C. Powerless

    ....

    ....

    ....

AFFIRMATIONS FOR SELF-CONTROL

I am a work in progress.
I am all there is.
I respect myself.
I am getting a dose of
Love and respect that is
Just for me.

How to Manage Your Anger

1. Anger does not have to be released like steam in a pressure cooker.

2. Venting/expressing your anger makes you feel better only for a moment, then regret, disappointment, and sorrow follow an emotional outburst.

3. The first step is to figure out what is causing you to get angry or react in an angry way.

    a. What are you saying to yourself inside your head?

    b. Do you feel taken advantage of, disrespected, ignored, used, not acknowledged?

    c. Do you have a fear of rejection?

    d. Do you like yourself?
    People who like themselves do not need to prove to someone else they are right.
    People who like themselves do not take or interpret things others say to them as a personal offense. They can give the other person the benefit of the doubt or let things pass without responding.

THE VALUE OF ANGER

Anger is a valuable signal, because it lets us know when something is wrong and needs to be corrected. The critical factor is whether your expression of anger is adding to the problem rather than solving the problem. You do not have a right to hurt others.

Often when we are angry, one or more of these things are going on:

1. We want something and are not getting it.
2. From past experience, we expect trouble.
3. We feel powerless to get what we want.

The principle of anger management techniques is for you to use your anger as a signal to *identify your problem/s and deal with it/them*; rather than act upon your anger by lashing out, and make the situation worse, or hold your angry feelings inside and let it become resentment.

ANGER CAN LEAD TO:

1. Angrily lashing out → to make the situation worse

2. Holding feelings inside → creates resentment, physical symptoms

OR

You can identify the problem to handle or solve it.

You do this by changing the thoughts you think. This is helpful when thinking about something that irritates you and makes you mad.

ACCEPTANCE

Acceptance is the answer to all my problems today.
When I am disturbed, it is because I find some person,
Place, thing or situation...some fact of my life
Unacceptable to me and I can find no serenity until I accept
that person, place or thing or situation as being exactly the
way it is suppose to be at this moment.
Nothing, absolutely nothing, happens in God's world by
Mistake; unless I accept life completely on life's terms I
Cannot be happy. I need to concentrate not so much on
What needs to be changed in the world as on what needs to
Be changed in me and in my attitudes.

When a situation provokes you and you are preparing to respond, Think and ask yourself some critical questions:

1. How can I manage this situation?
2. What is it that I absolutely have to do?
3. Decide how you will regulate your anger?
4. Will an argument between you and the other person solve your problem?
5. Do you have a plan for time to calm down or relax when angry?

Visualization Exercise To See Things Differently
Use this to see the other person's point of view.
1. Close your eyes.
2. Imagine you see a red apple.
3. Imagine yourself as a small child.
4. When you get the image, hold it, replace it with your new image, then, open your eyes.

ALTERNATIVES TO ANGRILY ACTING OUT:
Rethink, Change Your Expression of Anger, In Order To Change Your Thinking
Change what you say to yourself in your head, in response to the external event.
1. Take time to rethink about what has provoked you.
2. Use a planned relaxation technique
3. Stay calm and keep your cool
4. Ask yourself if you are overreacting, taking thing too seriously, or justifying your right to be angry.

ON REBELLION
Rebellion against your faults, shortcomings
and Handicaps, gets you nowhere.
Self-pity gets you nowhere.
One must have the adventure and
Daring to accept oneself
As a bundle of possibilities
And undertake the most
Interesting game in the world
Making the most of ones best

– HARRY EMERSON FREDRICK

Anger Management, Power vs. Control

1. **Power or control is the need to get attention, or energy.**

2. **We get attention in several ways; we can act as an:**
   A. Intimidator
   B. Interrogator
   C. Detached or aloof
   D. Acting like a victim

3. **What drama or chaos do you create in your family to get attention?**

   ....

   ....

4. **What do you do or how do you act to feel powerful? Are you one of these?**
   A. **Intimidators** – Threaten and frighten others
   B. **Interrogators** – Try to make others feel insecure by over powering them, belittling them or discrediting their judgment.
   C. **Detached or aloof** – Have people seeking them. to Find out what is wrong and why they are sad/mad.
   D. **Victim** – Play poor me and make others feel sorry for them to get attention and energy.

ANGER MANAGEMENT LOG

Name: ....Date:............

Fill out this log each time you find yourself in an anger-provoking situation.

1. What was the situation? Who was involved?
   ....
   ....

2. On a scale of 1 to 5, how angry was I? Write a number to show how you felt
   • Irritated
   • Embarrassed
   • Upset
   • Mad
   • Very Mad

3. What did you say or do to respond? ....
   ....
   ....

4. Was your response appropriate? ..... or inappropriate?.....
   Why? ....
   ....

5. What was the consequence of my response? Did I get what I wanted? ....

Child (signature): ....

Staff/Guardian (signature) ....

MYSELF

I have to live with myself, and so
I want to be fit for myself to know,
I want to be able, as days go by,
Always to look myself straight in the eye;
I don't want to stand, with the setting sun,
And hate myself for the things I've done.
I don't want to keep on a closet shelf,
a lot of secrets about myself.
And fool myself, as I come and go,
Into thinking that nobody else will know
The kind of person that I really am;
I don't want to dress up myself in a sham.
I want to go out with my head erect,
I want to deserve all men's respect;
But here in the struggle for fame and self,
I want to be able to like myself.
I don't want to look at myself and know
That I'm bluster and bluff and empty show,
I never can hide myself from me;
I see what others may never see;
I know what others may never know;
I never can fool myself, and so,
Whatever happens, I want to be
Self-respecting and conscience free.

— EDGAR A. GUEST

WHAT IS AN ANGER WORKOUT?

An Anger workout is a mental exercise to help you be and stay in control of yourself. The key point to remember is that your anger work-out, process is ongoing. We have to continually work out our frustration and anger, just like we work out our body muscles. When you stop doing any of the work-outs, your old counterproductive anger habits are likely to reemerge. The more you work out, the less chance there is others to be hurt by your old anger habits. Eventually, you will be able to do the work-outs on an automatic basis. When this happens you will be more productive in all aspects of your life. You will be: a more loving person, better: student, friend, associate, parent, more effective worker and live longer. Working out your anger shapes you up for live.

My prayer is that you live a long, stress free, fruitful life, and achieve all your goals and aspiration. Anger is neither good nor bad. It is just an emotion. When used wisely, it can allow you to be a powerful person, who is a pleasure to be around. I coach children, adults, entrepreneurs, and corporations on how to effectively communicate and negotiate to get what you desire.

You can reach me at:
> Tel.: 619-262-9951, or
> www.selfesteemcenter.org, or
> www.idagreene.com
> E-mail: idagreene@idagreene.com

We have several books to assist you, they are:
Anger Management Skills for Men
Anger Management Skills for Women
How to Improve Self-Esteem in Any Child
How to Improve Self-Esteem in the

African American Child
Self-Esteem the Essence of You
Light the Fire Within You
Soft Power Negotiation Skills
Money – How to Get It, How to Keep It
How to be a Success in Business
Are You Ready for Success?
*Say Goodbye to Your Smallness, Say Hello
    to Your Greatness*
    and
Stirring Up the African American Spirit.

Now You Keep Track of
When Someone Made You Mad
and How You Responded

CPSIA information can be obtained
at www.ICGtesting.com
Printed in the USA
LVOW08s0057291216
519060LV00002B/70/P

9 781881 165231